Introduction:

Stepdads are the unsung heroes of America. They are here to teach and to pick up slack. Sometimes their great knowledge is over looked because they are never as good as their wife's ex husband Rick who was more successful, more attractive and looked better with his shirt off...so my stepdad told me.
But nonetheless, The Funny Stepdad's book is filled with great photos and thoughts my stepdad once told me when I was growing up. Now you can enjoy them around a coffee table or mostly likely, on the toilet.

TheFunnyStepdad.com

THE FUNNY STEPDAD
"Life Lessons"
A coffee table book that you will read on the toilet.

By Tony Moser

Thanks to: My parents, Greg and Sandy for not judging me when I have thought of dumb things to do in my spare time.

Kim Johnson for being my girlfriend and not freaking out when looking at pictures of me with a creepy mustache.

Christie Jo Ray for taking my awesome pictures out in public without any fear.

All photos by:
Christie Jo Ray
Christie Jo Photography
Christiejophography@gmail.com
https://www.facebook.com/ChristieJoPhotography

Visit TheFunnyStepdad.com for more Stepdad stuff.

THE FUNNY STEPDAD

Deodorant.

A mid 40's man's cologne.

No ladies.

I'm not out of shape. That's baby fat.

COMUNITY COLEGE.

When you feel your just smart enough.

Doesn't believe in leap year.

Stepdad fact #71.

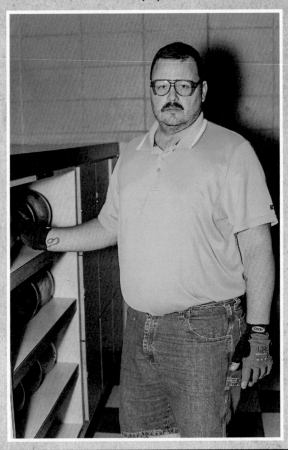

"Care for a cider?"

No because beer is still an option.

Crossfit.

Nope.

BOWLING.

The better you are the less you get laid.

"Diet and Exercise"
my doctor says.

In the same tone as if he said "ever heard of diet and exercise?"

The Funny Stepdad.

Spellcheck.

When you want to look ducking dumber when teching sun one.

TheFunnyStepdad.com

Superstores.

A place where you can buy meat and underwear.

Vacuuming.

Women's professional sports.

The bathroom.

The only place in the house you watch yourself drink water.

Eating crab.

It's like cleaning a hoarders house for a dollar.

-Some rewards aren't worth the work-

TheFunnyStepdad.com

The Funny Stepdad.

It's polite to say "Excuse me"

unless you say it loud.

Female condoms.

You ever put a new trash liner in a garbage can?

At night cover your feet with a blanket.

Just in case you have a ghost with a foot fetish.

Two teeth are still baby teeth.

Stepdad fact #77.

When someone gives you a high-five,

high-five back and yell "YES I AGREE AS WELL!"

Dog years.

This is stupid. Dogs don't understand math.

A grown man with earrings.

#12 of "things that should have an age limit"

The Funny Stepdad.

Ever accidentally pictured someone naked?

What about now?

TheFunnyStepdad.com

The Funny Stepdad.

Cremation.

When you wanna give your loved ones a lifetime chore.

-Moving a delicate item over and over can be fun-

TheFunnyStepdad.com

Piano Lessons.

Passive aggressive child abuse.

Was fired from the sophomore high school football team.

Stepdad fact #15.

Football season.

When alcoholism and eating like crap is demanded.

Football.

Drunk at 10am? No problem.

Fired?

More like get drunk and take a nap.

Lemon juice.

AKA, cut finders.

Gives 45%.

Every. Time.

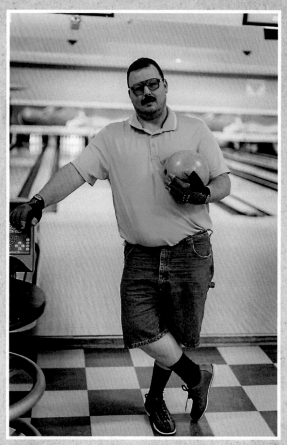

The dentist says I should be flossing.

Yeah. I should also be saving for retirement.

Pickles.

AKA, drunk cucumbers.

Feminism.

It's funny when people make up words.

Rodeo Bulls.

Maybe they aren't mean they're just hella germaphobes.

A grown man riding a racing bike on the streets.

#37 of "Things I don't trust".

Helen Keller once said

"   "

Accidently pissed on a hornets nest.

Stepdad fact #16.

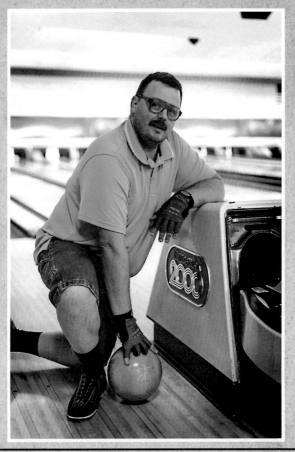

Once made my own shoe phone.

Stepdad fact #99.

Dogs.
Eats their own poop, no problem.
Eats a sliver of chocolate, dies.

Pizza Rolls.

A quicker Olive Garden.

Birds.

Always have diarrhea.

Hitler had a girlfriend.

I was single for 23 years. In a row.

The Funny Stepdad.

Likes VERY short walks on the beach.

Sleeping.

I'm self taught.

Milk.

Cow gland water.

UF YU CUN REED THIZ

THEN IT DUSNT MATER UF MI SPELNG IS BAD

Lawsuit.

White people karate.

GLUTEN FREE.

Learning cursive.

Thanks for wasting my fudging childhood.

Once interviewed at Target wearing a tank top.

Stepdad fact #34.

Never received a trophy.

Stepdad fact #23.

Women with armpit hair.

I'd rather see a puppy get murdered.

TheFunnyStepdad.com

Playing basketball.

#5 on the list of "Things I don't have confidence doing in public".

Honey.

AKA, Bee throw up.

The Funny Stepdad.

I'm not afraid of cops.

I'm afraid of paying fines.

TheFunnyStepdad.com

Oatmeal.

Adult baby throw up breakfast food.

O.C.D.

Forces me to eat the whole bag of pizza roles.

The Funny Stepdad.

Plus size models.

Only get attention if they aren't "face ugly".

TheFunnyStepdad.com

Push ups.

#86 of things I don't do in public.

Born again Christian.

AKA, spiritual bankruptcy.

Soccer.

For those who aren't man enough to play football.

Spellcheck.

Probably invented by some annoying nerd.

High school.

Something that can be learned in 3 Youtube videos.

Jumping Jacks.

Something only children should do.

We can talk to people in space,

but I can't get reception in my living room when it's raining.

Lemonade.

When you want to prove to someone you like lemonade.

The Funny Stepdad.

Breast feeding in public.

Equivalent to an old man kissing his adult son on the lips.

TheFunnyStepdad.com

The upstairs apartment.

When no one else matters.

TheFunnyStepdad.com

TOFU.

In Chinese means "effin' gross".

Vegans.

AKA, people I can beat up.

Wind and hamsters.

I don't know where either come from.

The Funny Stepdad.

Spelling.

One thing I need to improv on.

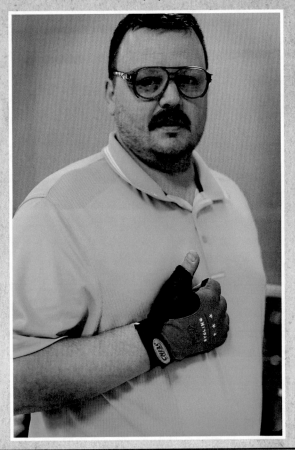

When all else fails...

give up and get drunk.

Tattoos.

When losing weight is too tough.

-It's like sweeping dirt under the couch-

Warm beer.

It's still beer.

Wine.

The ballet of booze.

Two women shaking hands.

I don't know why, but it's weird.

The Funny Stepdad.

High School tennis.

When your mom won't let you play football.

TheFunnyStepdad.com

Childhood.

The only time in your life when it's cool to lose your teeth.

The Funny Stepdad.

Only runs if life is in danger.

Stepdad fact #12.

TheFunnyStepdad.com

Racquetball.

AKA, Claustrophobic Hurt Tennis.

Fantasy Football.

Magic The Gathering for jocks.

Seagulls.

The douchebags of birds.

The Funny Stepdad.

Second Aid.

When you can't afford the 1st one.

TheFunnyStepdad.com

Soccer.

Women's hockey.

Texting.

When you say "frick it" to spelling.

Works out in jeans.

Makes the whole gym uncomfortable.

Never forget.

Wine is women's beer.

Drinks beer in the shower.

Getting clean the American way.

Work hard. Play hard.

I don't know what either of those mean.

Made in the USA
Columbia, SC
12 July 2017